GW01246634

PUFFIN FACTFINDEI

WONDERS
OF THE
WORLD

Written by
Fiona Corbridge

Edited by
Fiona Mitchell

PUFFIN BOOKS

The author, **Fiona Corbridge**, is a freelance writer and editor.

Consultants: **Keith Lye** is a well-known geographer and author of over 90 books for children. **Michael Allan** has a first class degree in Engineering from Heriot Watt University. He now works in engineering construction.

PUFFIN BOOKS

Published by the Penguin Group
Penguin Books Ltd, 27 Wrights Lane, London W8 5TZ, England
Penguin Books USA Inc., 375 Hudson Street, New York, New York 10014, USA
Penguin Books Australia Ltd, Ringwood, Victoria, Australia
Penguin Books Canada Ltd, 10 Alcorn Avenue, Toronto, Ontario, Canada M4V 3B2
Penguin Books (NZ) Ltd, 182-190 Wairau Road, Auckland 10, New Zealand

Penguin Books Ltd, Registered Offices: Harmondsworth, Middlesex, England

First published 1996
10 9 8 7 6 5 4 3 2 1

Produced for Puffin Books by Zigzag Publishing Ltd, The Barn, Randolph's Farm, Brighton Road, Hurstpierpoint, West Sussex, BN6 9EL, Britain.
Series concept: Tony Potter
Creative Manager: Hazel Songhurst
Managing Editor: Helen Burnford
Production by: Zoë Fawcett and Simon Eaton
Designed by: Ed Org
Illustrated by: Maureen Gray, Peter Bull, Mainline Design, Peter Dennis (Linda Rogers Assoc.).
Cover Design: Deborah Chadwick
Cover Illustration: Sîan Frances

Colour separations: RCS Graphics Ltd, Leeds
Printed by: Proost, Belgium

Contents

About this Book

This book is packed full of wonders from all over the world. There are natural wonders such as volcanoes, geysers, caves, tornadoes and comets; and incredible man-made wonders such as enormous statues, huge carvings and tunnels under the sea.

Find out about heads sculpted in a mountainside, a house that was first built with 18 rooms and ended with 160, and objects mysteriously turning into stone. Look at a lake that you can't sink in, massive towers and spectacular bridges and, read about the longest roller coaster in the world.

There are amazing constructions made of glass, structures made from skeletons, and ancient works of art. Discover the Seven Wonders of the Ancient World, the Channel Tunnel, Stonehenge, Pompeii, Walt Disney World and much more in this fascinating look at the extraordinary wonders of our world.

The Wonders of the Ancient World

In the second century BC, a Greek man called Antipater of Sidon decided to write about seven of the most marvellous structures that existed at the time. These became known as the Seven Wonders of the Ancient World.

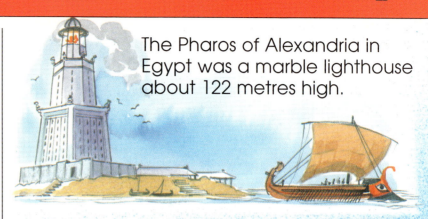

The Pharos of Alexandria in Egypt was a marble lighthouse about 122 metres high.

The pyramids of Giza in Egypt were the tombs of Ancient Egyptian kings and queens. They were buried with all the things they thought they might need in their next life, such as food, furniture and jewels.

The statue of Zeus, King of the Greek gods, was carved from ivory and marble. It was 12 metres tall and built at Olympia, Greece.

The Ancient Greeks built temples to worship gods and goddesses. The Temple of Artemis, in Ephesus, Turkey, was built to worship the goddess of hunting and fertility.

King Mausolus decided to build himself the grandest tomb in the world at Halicarnassus, Turkey. A new word was invented to describe the tomb – mausoleum, after Mausolus.

The biggest pyramid at Giza is about 146 metres high, and is made of over two million blocks of stone.

The Colossus of Rhodes was a huge bronze statue of the Sun god, Helios. It was 37 metres high, and stood on the Mediterranean island of Rhodes.

King Nebuchadnezzar built the beautiful Hanging Gardens of Babylon in Mesopotamia for his wife. Stone terraces were shaped like pyramids and filled with colourful plants.

Building Wonders

Amazing buildings are found all over the world. There are wonderful castles and palaces, strange houses, and very unusual shops!

In Houston, US, a shop has been designed to look as though it is falling down!

Neuschwanstein Castle

In Germany in 1869, King Ludwig of Bavaria began building himself a fairytale castle with lots of towers and turrets.

Imagine a huge building made completely of glass. Crystal Palace was built in London, UK in 1851. Its great iron frame contained 300,000 pieces of glass.

In Beijing, China, the Emperor lived in his own private city, with palaces, lakes and gardens. Ordinary people were not allowed in, so it was called the Forbidden City.

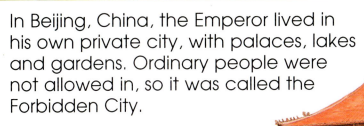

The Biosphere, in the Arizona desert, US, was like a huge greenhouse, containing different habitats, each with plants and animals.

The Palace of Versailles in France is 580 metres long and is the biggest palace in the world. It was built for King Louis XIV in 1682.

The Biosphere experiment was set up to see if people could survive on what they could grow within the building. Volunteers had to stay inside for two years.

One of the strangest houses in the world is in California, US. Its owner, Sarah Winchester, was afraid of ghosts and believed that they would harm her unless she kept doing building work on the house. Work went on for 38 years!

It has weird features such as staircases which lead nowhere.

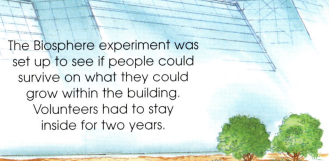

The house started with 18 rooms and ended with 160!

Mountains are made when rocks under the Earth's surface move. Sometimes molten rock rises up inside the Earth and pushes the land into a dome shape.

Some mountains are volcanoes. A volcano is a hole in the Earth's surface. Hot molten rock (lava) inside the Earth shoots out of the hole when the volcano erupts.

Ayers Rock in Australia is the biggest rock in the world. It is 2.5 kilometres long and 348 metres high.

From the rocky desert of Monument Valley in Utah, US, strange towering chunks of rock rise to 300 metres. Water, wind and temperature changes have worn away the surrounding rock to make shapes that look like ruined castles or crumbling skyscrapers.

The largest active volcano is Mauna Loa, in Hawaii. An active volcano is one that still erupts. Mauna Loa last erupted in 1984.

One of the biggest and most terrifying volcanic eruptions was when Krakatoa in Indonesia exploded in 1883. Rock shot 25 kilometres into the air, and dust fell over 5000 kilometres away.

Krakatoa

When Mount Vesuvius in Italy erupted in AD 79, the Roman town of Pompeii was completely buried by volcanic ash. When archaeologists dug out the town centuries later they found that the buildings and beautiful mosaics had been preserved by the lava.

The highest mountain in the world is Mount Everest, in the Himalayan mountains. It is 8848 metres high. The first people to climb to the top were Edmund Hillary and Sherpa Tenzing Norgay, in 1953.

The longest range of mountains is the Andes in South America. It stretches for about 7600 kilometres.

Towering Wonders

Many tall buildings are built with a frame made from steel and concrete. Others are built around a huge hollow concrete tube.

Builders dig deep into the ground to make a support for the building, called the foundations.

The world's most famous tower looks as if it will fall over! The Leaning Tower of Pisa, in Italy, was finished in 1350. It is 56 metres high. Because the soft ground has sunk under the tower, it leans over 4 metres to one side.

Alexandre-Gustave Eiffel built the world's tallest tower for the Paris Exhibition of 1889.

The Eiffel Tower, Paris, France is 300 metres high, made of iron girders held together by rivets.

Built in 1931, the Empire State Building in New York City, US, appeared in a famous film. Using trick photography, a fierce giant ape called King Kong was shown clinging to the top of the 381-metre skyscraper.

Lighthouses warn ships where there is danger from underwater rocks. The tallest lighthouse in Britain is Bishop Rock, near the Scilly Isles. It is 49 metres high.

The tallest tower in the world today is the CN Tower in Toronto, Canada. It is 553.34 metres high. From its revolving restaurant you can see for 120 kilometres.

More than 62,000 tonnes of earth was excavated for the CN Tower's foundations.

The Chrysler Building, New York, US, is one of the world's most beautiful skyscrapers. Some of its design was based on a rising sun and parts of a Chrysler car!

Since ancient times, people have sculpted images of humans and gods. Some are carved from stone or wood, or cast from metal. Many of them are enormous.

In Ancient Britain, people carved giant figures and animals into chalky hillsides. The 'Long Man' at Wilmington, East Sussex is 68 metres long – the largest hill carving in Britain.

An enormous statue of Jesus overlooks Rio de Janeiro in Brazil. The sculptor, Paul Landowski, built the 40-metre tall concrete statue in 1931.

On Easter Island in the South Pacific Ocean, hundreds of strange stone figures were discovered. Archaeologists think they were carved some time between AD 1000 and 1600.

In 1257 BC, an Egyptian pharaoh decided to build a great temple at Abu Simbel. It had four 20-metre tall statues of the pharaoh, Ramesses II, at the entrance.

The tallest statue in the world stands in Tokyo, Japan. This bronze statue of Buddha is 120 metres tall and weighs 1000 tonnes.

One man turned a mountainside into a sculpture! Gutzon Borglum carved the heads of four American presidents on Mount Rushmore in South Dakota, US. It took him 14 years.

In 1501, the artist Michelangelo carved a beautiful lifelike marble statue of David, who killed the giant Goliath in the Bible story. It was sculpted out of a huge marble block which a sculptor had worked on years before, but had abandoned. Michelangelo designed his sculpture to fit into the chiselled marble block. The statue is over twice life-size.

A waterfall is formed when a river wears away the soft rock beneath a layer of hard rock to form a step.

Geysers are caused when water is heated by hot rocks under the ground. Steam pressure builds up and forces a jet of hot water out of a hole in the ground.

The highest waterfall in the world is the Angel Falls in Venezuela. It drops 979 metres.

One of the most famous waterfalls in the world is the Victoria Falls on the River Zambezi in Africa. Visitors have a great view of the Falls from cliffs just 75 metres away.

The Great Barrier Reef off Queensland in Australia is the biggest coral reef in the world. It is a rock-like mass built up from tiny sea creatures called corals and their skeletons.

Many sea urchins, oysters and colourful fish live on the Reef.

The tallest ever geyser shot out hot, black water and huge rocks to a height of 460 metres. The Waimangu Geyser in New Zealand used to erupt about every three days, but has been quiet since 1904.

Today, the tallest geyser is in Yellowstone National Park in Wyoming, US. Known as the Steamboat Geyser, its eruptions reach heights of up to 115 metres.

On his way to California, US, in 1933, a sailor saw the highest ever recorded wave during a hurricane. It was 34 metres tall.

The strongest sea currents in the world reach a speed of 30 kilometres per hour in the Nakwakto Rapids, British Columbia in Canada.

Tunnels carry roads and railways beneath cities, through mountains and under the sea. Some tunnels supply water, and others take away sewage.

Tunnels may be cut out of rock by huge boring machines. Some tunnels are built in sections and then buried.

Tunnels allow canals to pass through hills. Up until the mid-1900s, canal boats were guided through tunnels by men called 'leggers'.

The Channel Tunnel is the world's longest tunnel under the sea. It travels 50 kilometres under the English Channel from England to France.

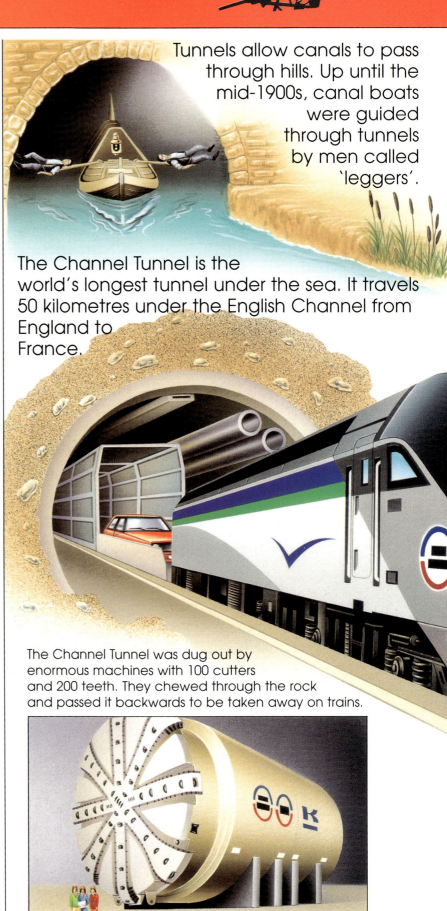

The Channel Tunnel was dug out by enormous machines with 100 cutters and 200 teeth. They chewed through the rock and passed it backwards to be taken away on trains.

It took 24 years for engineers to build the world's longest rail tunnel. The Seikan Tunnel in Japan is 53.85 kilometres long. It joins two islands by passing 100 metres below the sea-bed.

The tunnels of the gold mine at Carletonville in South Africa are 3581 metres under the ground, making it the deepest mine in the world. Every day, over 11,000 miners dig out the gold.

In Switzerland, the St. Gotthard Tunnel burrows through mountains called the Alps. Measuring 16.32 kilometres, this is the longest road tunnel in the world.

Deep under the city, the tube trains of the London Underground in England rumble through 171 kilometres of tunnels. This is the biggest underground railway in the world.

Entertaining Wonders

Throughout history, people have created magnificent structures for entertainments.

Sydney Opera House overlooks Sydney harbour in Australia. It is shaped like a series of shells and is covered in tiles which catch the light. There are five separate halls inside.

Las Vegas, US, has lots of buildings decorated with neon lights.

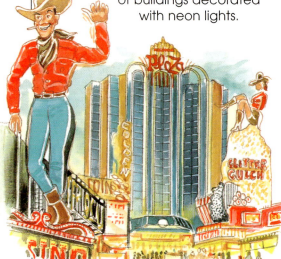

The Romans built the Colosseum in Rome, Italy. It was a huge sporting arena. Up to 50,000 people would come to watch gladiators fight.

Walt Disney World in Florida, US, is the biggest amusement park in the world. It takes five days to look round all of it!

The longest roller coaster ride in the world is at Lightwater Valley Theme Park in Yorkshire, UK. It is over 2 kilometres long.

In Ancient Greece, open-air theatres were very popular. At Epidaurus theatre, 14,000 people could watch a play. Actors on stage could be heard even if you sat right at the top.

The four-storey Colosseum can still be seen in Rome. It is 56 metres high, and measures 527 metres round.

The biggest football stadium in the world is in Rio de Janeiro in Brazil. It can hold a crowd of 205,000 people.

The Superdome in New Orleans, US, is the largest indoor stadium in the world. In Toronto, Canada, SkyDome Stadium, pictured below, has the biggest moving roof in the world. It is rolled back in summer.

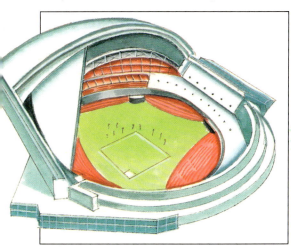

Southend Pier in Essex, UK, is the longest pier in the world. The stroll along it is 2.15 kilometres. Since it was built in 1830, 14 ships have crashed into it!

Caves are formed when rainwater gradually wears away rock, and streams work their way underground. The streams form tunnels which slowly grow into caves.

In the Cueva de Nerja, Málaga, Spain, hangs a 59-metre stalactite – the longest in the world. The tallest stalagmite in the world is in the Krásnohorská cave in Slovakia. It is 32 metres tall.

In Kentucky, US, explorers have found the biggest collection of connected caves in the world. The Mammoth Cave system covers 560 kilometres.

The deepest cave in the world is at Réseau Jean Bernard in France. It is 1602 metres deep.

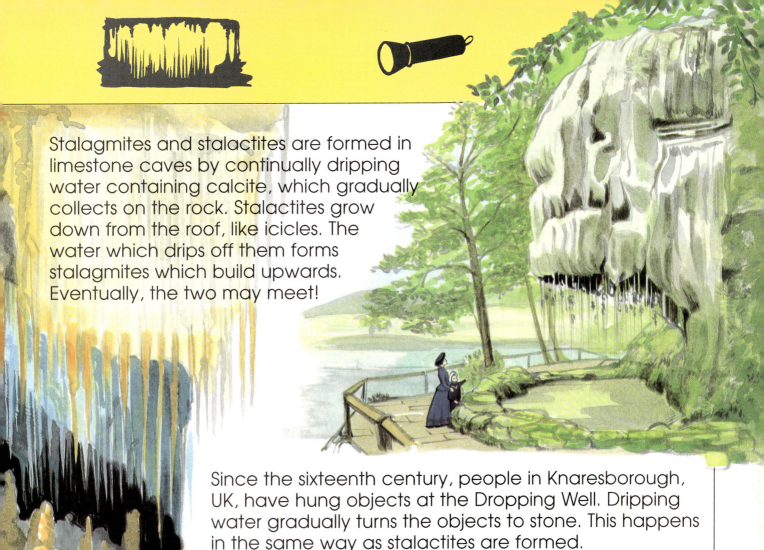

Stalagmites and stalactites are formed in limestone caves by continually dripping water containing calcite, which gradually collects on the rock. Stalactites grow down from the roof, like icicles. The water which drips off them forms stalagmites which build upwards. Eventually, the two may meet!

Since the sixteenth century, people in Knaresborough, UK, have hung objects at the Dropping Well. Dripping water gradually turns the objects to stone. This happens in the same way as stalactites are formed.

The biggest underwater cave is in Mexico. Divers have explored 39,480 metres of passages in the Nohoch Na Chich caves.

At 700 metres long and 300 metres wide, with a roof at least 70 metres high, the biggest cave in the world is the Sarawak Chamber, Lubang Nasib Bagus, in Sarawak, Malaysia.

Religious Wonders

There have been many religions in the history of the world. Since ancient times people have believed in one or many gods.

Often impressive structures have been built as places of worship.

In the Far East, Buddhists build tower-shaped temples called pagodas. This wooden Japanese pagoda in Kyoto was built in the seventh century.

In Wiltshire, UK, the massive stones of ancient Stonehenge stand in a circle. Nobody really knows what they were for, but they may have been used for religious ceremonies. Stonehenge could be over 4,000 years old.

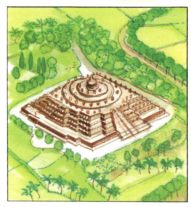

The Buddhist Temple of Borobudur in Indonesia is built in huge layers of steps. There are 72 bell-shaped shrines on them, each containing a statue of the Buddha. It is the largest Buddhist temple in the world.

Angkor Wat is the biggest place of worship in the world. It is a Hindu temple in Cambodia built in the twelfth century. The carved stone towers and passageways cover 1.62 square kilometres.

The architect Antoni Gaudí started work on the Cathedral of the Sagrada Familia (Barcelona, Spain) in 1883, but it remains unfinished. Its fantastic spires are over 106 metres tall.

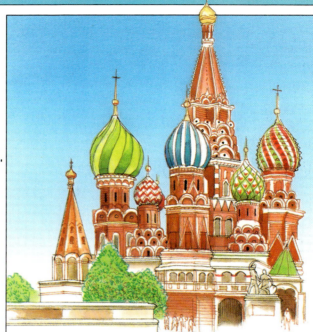

In Moscow, Russia, the towers of St. Basil's Cathedral look as though they are topped with many different coloured sweets!

The Great Mosque at Mecca in Saudi Arabia is visited by many Muslim pilgrims. This vast mosque was built in the seventh century. At the centre of its huge open courtyard is a holy shrine.

The Golden Temple at Amritsar in India is the most holy shrine of the Sikh religion. This beautiful golden building glistens in the sunlight. Inside, it is richly decorated with elaborate paintings and gold.

Artistic Wonders

Artists have created exciting works of art in many different forms, from painting and sculpture to textiles and glass.

One of the earliest ways to decorate walls was by mosaic. Using tiny pieces of glass, stone or marble, artists put together colourful pictures like amazing jigsaw puzzles.

The oldest artistic wonders date back to 30,000 BC, when Palaeolithic people created cave pictures using mineral powder.

The first cartoon strip in the world was embroidered in wool in the eleventh century! The Bayeux Tapestry tells the story of how the French conquered England in 1066. It is 70 metres long.

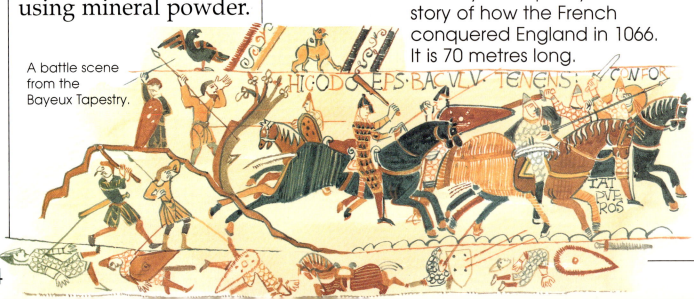

A battle scene from the Bayeux Tapestry.

This mosaic of the Empress Theodora is in a church in Ravenna, Italy. It was made in the sixth century AD.

Pablo Picasso produced more works of art during his life than any other artist. When Picasso died at the age of 78 in 1973, he had created around 148,000 pieces. His cubist paintings show several views of an object at the same time.

Stained glass windows in Christian churches were used to teach people about the Bible. This window in Cologne Cathedral in Germany tells the story of Jonah and the whale.

The most famous painting in the world is probably the *Mona Lisa*, which was painted by the Italian artist, Leonardo da Vinci, in about 1503.

It is said that music was played at every sitting for the portrait, so that the mysterious smile would not fade from the model's face.

25

Wherever the weather is very hot, dry or cold, the landscape displays incredible features. Canyons or gorges are valleys with steep rock walls.

The biggest glacier in the world is the Lambert Glacier in Antarctica, which is over 700 kilometres long. The fastest-moving glacier is in Alaska, and can move about 20 metres a day.

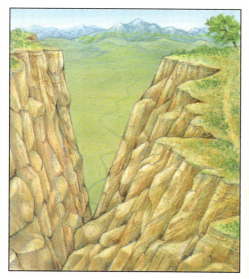

The Vicos Gorge in Greece is 1,100 metres wide and 900 metres deep.

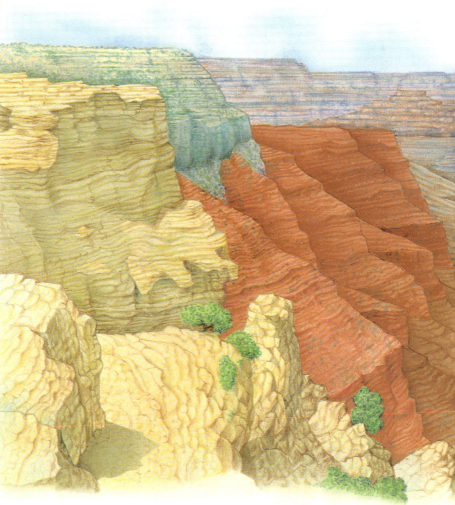

A glacier is a huge, slow-moving river of ice.

The biggest gorge in the world is the Grand Canyon, Arizona, US. It is about 16 kilometres wide and 446 kilometres long.

Visitors to Death Valley in California, US must be careful of the extreme heat. Sometimes it gets as hot as 52 °C.

The shores of the Dead Sea in Israel are 400 metres below sea-level. This is the lowest point on land in the world. The Dead Sea is the saltiest lake in the world. It has so much salt that you can't sink in it.

The largest desert in the world is the Sahara in North Africa. It spreads over 9 million square kilometres. The biggest sand dunes can be found in the Sahara. They rise to 465 metres.

In 1956, a survey ship sighted the biggest ever iceberg in the South Pacific Ocean. It was 335 kilometres long and 97 kilometres wide. Icebergs are huge chunks of ice which have broken off glaciers or ice sheets and entered the sea.

Engineering Wonders

Engineering is work that uses scientific knowledge for designing and building machines, vehicles, buildings, roads and structures such as bridges, dams and walls.

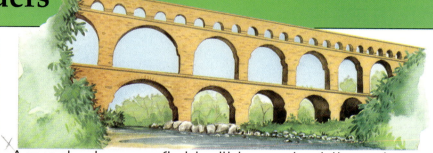

Aqueducts were first built in ancient times to carry water over a distance into towns. The Romans built the longest, which ran to the city of Carthage in Tunisia from springs 141 kilometres away.

Work on Britain's longest wall was started by the Romans in AD 122. Hadrian's Wall took only four years to build, and snaked 118 kilometres across northern England.

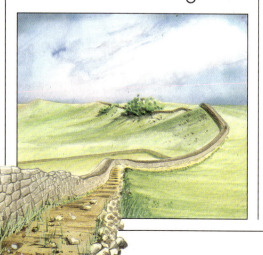

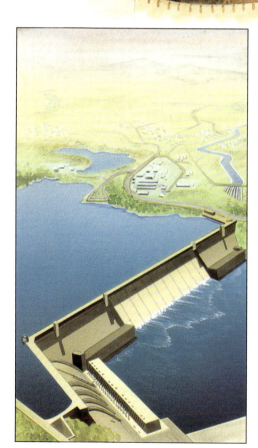

The most concrete ever used to build a dam was poured into the huge Grand Coulee Dam in Washington State, US. It is 1272 metres long and 167 metres high.

In the US, trains trundle 19 kilometres along the longest railway viaduct in the world. The viaduct crosses the Great Salt Lake in Utah.

Suspension bridges hang from cables between two towers. The Humber Estuary Bridge in Humberside, UK, is the longest in the world. The distance between its towers is 1410 metres.

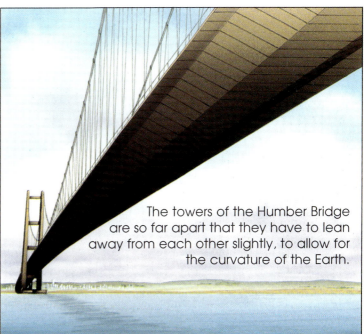

The towers of the Humber Bridge are so far apart that they have to lean away from each other slightly, to allow for the curvature of the Earth.

Sydney Harbour Bridge in Australia is the widest bridge in the world. At 48.8 metres wide, it carries two railway tracks, eight lanes of road, a cycle path and a footway.

The longest wall in the world can be seen from Space! The Great Wall of China stretches 3460 kilometres along a mountain range. The wall was built to keep invaders out of China. Builders worked for over a hundred years to finish it in about 210 BC.

A phenomenon is any remarkable occurrence. Natural phenomena are those which occur in nature.

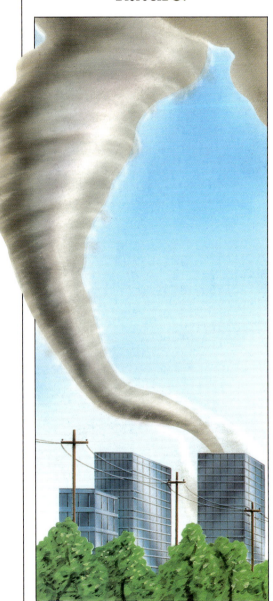

A tornado looks like a tube reaching out of a cloud. Its spiralling winds may reach 500 kilometres per hour.

A comet is a rocky object which travels around the Sun and can periodically be seen from Earth. Halley's Comet was first recorded in 240 BC.

A waterspout is a tornado which has formed over water, and created a tall spinning column of watery mist. The highest waterspout reached 1528 metres off New South Wales, Australia, in 1898.

A mirage is the illusion of a distant object or a sheet of water. It is caused by atmospheric conditions in hot weather.

A solar eclipse is when the Moon passes between the Sun and the Earth. The longest solar eclipse in recent times was in 1715, and lasted four minutes.

Meteorites are broken bits of comets or asteroids which fall to Earth. The biggest one ever found was 2.7 metres long and weighed 59 tonnes. It was found in Namibia, Africa, in 1920.

Hailstones form when water droplets in storm clouds freeze and fall to Earth. The heaviest hailstones fell in Bangladesh in 1986. They weighed a kilogramme and killed 92 people.

The northern lights, or aurora borealis, are different coloured bands of light that move across the sky in the polar region. They are caused by particles from the Sun reaching the Earth's magnetic field.

St. Elmo's fire is a luminous area which may appear around objects such as church spires, ships' masts, or aircraft wings. It is caused by electricity in the atmosphere.

 # Index